Camila CABELLO

Joanne Mattern

A ROBBIE READER

PUBLISHERS

2001 SW 31st Avenue
Hallandale, FL 33009

www.mitchelllane.com

First Edition, 2020.
Author: Joanne Mattern
Designer: Ed Morgan
Editor: Lisa Petrillo

Series: Robbie Reader
Title: Camila Cabello / by Joanne Mattern

Hallandale, FL : Mitchell Lane Publishers, [2020]

Library bound ISBN: 9781680205107
eBook ISBN: 9781680205114

Contents

Breaking Free

Camila Cabello had a big decision to make. For three years, she had been a part of Fifth Harmony. The five young women had come together on a talent show to create one of the best-selling female singing groups in history. But Cabello had had enough.

Fifth Harmony from left: Camila Cabello, Dinah Jane, Normani Kordei, Ally Brooke Hernandez, and Lauren Jauregui in December 2010

Cabello was not happy that Fifth Harmony singers did not write their own songs. Everything they did was programmed by their manager and their record company. Cabello had already worked solo singing with major musical artists including Shawn Mendes and Machine Gun Kelly. Now it was time for her to leave Fifth Harmony and strike out on her own.

Cabello did not want her exit to cause a lot of drama. But that is exactly what happened. The other four young women in Fifth Harmony were hurt and angry. In December 2016, they announced that Cabello had left the group without telling them first. Cabello responded that the other women knew she was unhappy and planning to leave. Cabello wrote, "I did not intend to end things with Fifth Harmony this way." Soon the conversation turned into an argument that spread through social media. Fifth Harmony's fans were angry, upset, and confused

Even though she did not like the drama, Cabello knew that leaving Fifth Harmony was the right things to do. "The easiest route would be to shut my mouth, sing the songs, wear the clothes, and keep going," Cabello told a reporter for *Billboard* magazine. "We were at the peak of our career. It's definitely not the safe option. But I have it in my DNA. The way my mom raised me, it has always been: Don't settle. Jump and hope you grow wings on the way down."

Leaving Fifth Harmony was a difficult decision. When she left, Cabello was not sure what the future held. She would soon learn that her life was about to get even better.

Fifth Harmony at Radio Disney Music Awards in L.A. April 2015

Overcoming Obstacles

Karla Camila Cabello Estrabao was born March 3, 1997, in Havana, Cuba. Camila's parents, Alejandro and Sinuhe, moved the family back and forth between Havana and Mexico City. When Camila was six years old, she and her mother moved to Miami, Florida. Her father moved to Miami 18 months later. Camila also has a younger sister named Sofia.

At first, Camila suffered from stage fright but worked hard to share her music with fans.

Life in Miami was hard. Camila's father washed cars for a living. Her mother stocked shoes in a department store. "My parents worked really hard," Camila told a *Billboard* reporter. "We always had periods when my dad would be out of a job. It was a constant flow of having money, losing everything, and then finding a way to get it again." Later, Camila's parents were able to start a successful construction business, and life got easier.

Camila always loved to sing and perform. In 2014, she told her high-school newspaper, the *Palmetto Panther*, "I've loved music since I can remember, but I always brushed it off as a hobby that I should keep to myself. It was this wild daydream that I believed I could never actually achieve."

To make matters worse, Camila had a terrible case of stage fright. She would even cry when her parents asked her to sing for them. Finally, Camila realized that if she wanted to be a singer, she had to fight her fears. "I decided I wasn't going to let fear stop me from living a life I was passionate about. I decided to audition just to see if I was good, and that's all it takes—five seconds of bravery to change your whole life."

Camila decided to face her fears in a big way. In 2012, she heard that the TV show *The X Factor* was holding auditions. She begged her parents to drive her from Florida to North Carolina to try out. The trip was Camila's fifteenth-birthday present. It was a trip that would change her life.

Camila worked hard to find the self-confidence
to sing onstage.

The
X Factor
Battle

Cabello's X Factor journey did not start out well. Before she could go before the judges, she had to audition for **producers**. At first, Cabello was not picked to appear before the judges. Instead, she was asked to be an **alternate**.

For 48 hours, Cabello and her family waited and worried. Finally, Cabello was picked to **audition** before Simon Cowell and the other judges. She told *Seventeen* magazine, "I ended up auditioning because they saw how badly I wanted it and how **persistent** I was."

The judges liked what they saw, even Cowell who was famous for often being mean to performers. Cabello got four yeses from the judges. She moved on to the "boot camp" part of the **competition**. During this time, contestants work on their songs and perform before the judges.

At the end of boot camp, Cabello faced another disappointment. She was not chosen to continue in the competition. Then, Cowell had a change of heart. Instead of singing as a solo artist, he asked Cabello to join four other girls on the show. Together, they became the group Fifth Harmony.

Simon Cowell with Fifth Harmony in December 2012.

Cabello was thrilled at the chance. "I was so excited that it wasn't over because I wanted to just keep going on that journey," she told *Seventeen*. "It was so new and exciting to me, and I was like a kid in a candy store." Cabello and the other four girls—Ally Brooke, Normani Kordei, Lauren Jauregui, and Dinah Jane—became friends as they worked together and moved on in the competition.

Fifth Harmony ended up coming in third place on *The X Factor*. Even though they did not win, their journey was not over. Simon Cowell signed the group to his company, Syco Music. The group also got a record deal with Epic Records. For Cabello and her new friends, big things were about to happen.

Jennel Garcia, Demi Lovato, Paige Thomas, Simon Cowell, and Fifth Harmony onstage at *The X Factor* Live Elimination Show in November 2012.

Fifth Harmony *Takes Off*

Fifth Harmony got right to work in the recording studio. In 2013, the group released an **EP** called *Better Together*. The EP reached number six on the *Billboard* Hot 200 Chart, which was a great success for a brand-new act.

In February 2015, Fifth Harmony released its first full-length album. It was called *Reflection*. *Reflection* **debuted** at number five on the Hot 200 Chart and was a hit around the world. The third single from the album, a song called "Worth It," became Fifth Harmony's biggest hit so far.

Fifth Harmony at the 2015 Billboard Music Awards at MGM Grand Garden Arena in May 2015.

Cabello and the other teenaged group members were thrilled that the song was a big hit, but they had not expected it. "We love the song, but we were kind of surprised, to be honest," fellow Fifth Harmony singer Normani Kordei told a *Billboard* reporter. That year, Fifth Harmony was named "Group of the Year" at the *Billboard* Women in Music Awards.

CHAPTER FOUR

In 2016, Fifth Harmony's third album, *7/27*, burst out with the hit single "Working From Home." Cabello was a big part of all the Fifth Harmony songs. She sang lead on almost half of the tunes. The group's fans, called Harmonizers, loved Cabello.

The group also toured around the world. Living and working with the other four members was a learning experience for Cabello. *The X Factor* "was the most intense experience of our lives," she told the *Palmetto Panther*. "We could not get through it if we did not have each other. Being in the group has taught me a lot about loyalty, about acceptance, and about what friendship really is. We spend more time with each other than we do our own families, which makes it feel like we're sisters. At the end of the day we're all we have and if anybody messes with any of them, I will always fight for them and protect them."

Cabello and the other members of Fifth Harmony pose for a friendly selfie. The group became close while working together.

Solo Success

Cabello's time in Fifth Harmony taught her a lot. Her manager, Roger Gold, said, "Fifth Harmony worked incredibly hard eleven-and-a-half months of the year. It was an incredible school."

But Cabello wanted more. She had always made it clear that she wanted to write her own songs and record with other artists. In 2015, she wrote and recorded "I Know What You Did Last Summer" with Shawn Mendes. The song was a huge hit. In 2016, Cabello had another hit with "Bad Things," a duet with rap singer Machine Gun Kelly.

Machine Gun Kelly and Cabello perform at
Y100's Jingle Ball 2016.

Cabello's solo work created some bad feelings with the other members of Fifth Harmony and their manager. As Cabello explained to a reporter for the *New York Times*, "It became clear that it was not possible to do solo stuff and be in the group at the same time."

Although her breakup with Fifth Harmony did not go as smoothly as she had hoped, Cabello never looked back. Instead, she released the single "Crying in the Club" and went on tour as the opening act for the star musician Bruno Mars.

On August 3, 2017, Cabello released her new song, "Havana." At first, no one thought the song would make a good single. However, it became a No. 1 hit around the world. By June 2018, "Havana" had become Spotify music website's most-streamed song by a solo female. The song's success gave Cabello a new confidence. "Nobody really knows anything, so you might as well go with what you love," she told a reporter for the British music magazine *NME*.

Cabello and her backup dancers perform
a fiery *Havana* in September 2017.

Cabello also believes in giving back to the community. In 2016, she partnered with Save the Children, a global charity dedicated to giving children a healthy start and protection during crisis. Part of her contribution was to design a special T-shirt. Sales of Cabello's shirt were donated to create educational and health-care opportunities for girls. Cabello has also worked with the Children's Health Fund to provide health care to low-income families with children. And in 2017, Cabello performed with famous Broadway playwright and performer Lin-Manuel Miranda in a special celebrity-filled recording of his song, "Almost Like Praying," The song helped raise money for victims of Hurricane Maria that devastated Puerto Rico.

Save The Children
Children's Health Fund
Hurricane Maria

Cabello knows she is a role model for people around the world. "I definitely feel a responsibility to be as best a person as possible for our younger fans," she told her high school newspaper. She encourages young people to follow their dreams. "Feel the fear and do it anyway. Believe in yourself. Love yourself. Root for yourself. Know that at the end of the day your life is yours, not your parents' or your friends' or your boyfriend's or your girlfriend's. You have to do what makes you happy because you're really all you got."

Cabello connects with her fans and advises them to "believe in yourself. Love yourself."

Timeline

1997   Camila Cabello is born March 3 in Havana, Cuba.

2003   Cabello and her mother move to Miami, Florida.

2012   Cabello auditions for *The X Factor* and becomes part of Fifth Harmony.

2013   Fifth Harmony releases *Better Together*, and it becomes a hit.

2015   Fifth Harmony releases *Reflection*; Cabello releases a song with Shawn Mendes.

2016   Fifth Harmony releases *7/27*; Cabello releases a song with Machine Gun Kelly; Cabello leaves Fifth Harmony.

2017   Cabello's song, "Havana," becomes a No. 1 hit.

Find Out More

Websites

Camila Cabello
http://www.camilacabello.com

"15 Facts You Need to Know About Fifth Harmony"
https://www.capitalxtra.com/features/lists/fifth-harmony-facts/

Fifth Harmony
http://fifthharmony.com

"21 Geeky Facts About Camila Cabello"
https://www.nme.com/blogs/camila-cabello-facts-2252388

Works Consulted

Arguelles, Victoria. "Q&A With Palmetto Student Camila Cabello." *The Palmetto Panther*, November 25, 2014. https://www.thepalmettopanther.com/qa-with-palmetto-student-camila-cabello/

Devoe, Noelle. "Camila Cabello Admits She Was Initially Rejected By '*X Factor*' Producers." Seventeen.com, January 10, 2017. https://www.seventeen.com/celebrity/movies-tv/news/a44357/camila-cabello-interview-x-factor-rejection/

Elizabeth, De. "Camila Cabello Opens Up About Fifth Harmony and Her Childhood." Teen Vogue, February 16, 2017. https://www.teenvogue.com/story/camila-cabello-opens-up-fifth-harmony-childhood

Halperin, Shirley. "Inside Camila Cabello's Fifth Harmony Exit: Where Did It All Go Wrong?" Billboard.com, December 21, 2016. https://www.billboard.com/articles/columns/pop/7632422/camila-cabello-fifth-harmony-exit-inside

Johnson, Zach. "Camila Cabello 'Shocked' Over How Fifth Harmony Handled Her Exit." E!News.com, December 19, 2016. https://www.eonline.com/news/816925/camila-cabello-shocked-over-how-fifth-harmony-handled-her-exit

Works Consulted continued

Levine, Nick. "The Big Interview: Camila Cabello on Total Control, Chasing a Buzz, and Why She Won't Be Doing Fifth Harmony Tunes Live." NME.com, February 2, 2018. https://www.nme.com/music-interviews/big-interview-camila-cabello-2018-2227094

Lipschutz, Jason. "Fifth Harmony 'Kind of Surprised' That 'Worth It' is Now Their Biggest Hit." Billboard.com, July 24, 2015. https://www.billboard.com/articles/columns/pop-shop/6641998/fifth-harmony-worth-it-podcast-interview

Martins, Chris. "Camila Cabello: Gone Girl." Billboard.com. https://features.billboard.com/camila-cabello-talks-solo-music-life-after-fifth-harmony/

Ugwu, Reggie. "How Camila Cabello Lost Some Friends and Found Her Voice." New York Times.com, January 11, 2018. https://www.nytimes.com/2018/01/11/arts/music/camila-cabello-fifth-harmony-solo-album.html

Villafañe, Veronica. "Lin-Manuel Miranda Releases Star-Studded 'Almost Like Praying' Song for Puerto Rico Hurricane Relief." Forbes.com, October 6, 2017. https://www.forbes.com/sites/veronicavillafane/2017/10/06/lin-manuel-miranda-releases-star-studded-almost-like-praying-song-for-puerto-rico-hurricane-relief/#12189fcf56b3

Glossary

alternate
A person who fills in if someone cannot complete a performance

audition
Trying out for a part in a movie, play, or TV show

competition
A contest

debuted
Appeared for the first time

EP
"Extended play" is a record album that contains only a few songs

persistent
Continuing in spite of difficulties

producers
People who supervise the making of a TV show, movie, or recording

Index

About the Author

Joanne Mattern enjoys writing celebrity biographies. She was drawn to writing about Camila Cabello because her daughters have admired this talented singer ever since her days with Fifth Harmony. Mattern has written many books for children, including numerous biographies for Mitchell Lane publishers. She lives in New York State with her husband, four children, and several pets.